Confident

Career Woman

Confident

Career Woman

Ditch Perfection, Play Bigger and Make PowHer Moves

ERICKA SPRADLEY

ISBN-13: 9781979507523
ISBN-10: 197950752X

Dear Confident Career Woman,

I believe women are truly one of God's greatest creations. I say this not because I'm a woman, but because of what I've read, experienced and observed. For more than two decades, I've watched women respond to the question "Who are you" by sharing who they are in relationship to someone else (I'm a mother, wife, etc.) and/or by communicating their profession. While these aspects of our lives are important, know that you are so much more and that the "more" is the basis for your competitive advantage.

Statistically speaking, working women surveyed between the ages of 25-64 believe the following will drive their careers forward according to KPMG Women's Leadership Study:

- Being confident in their abilities (75%)
- Asking for what they deserve (67%)
- Not allowing their gender to limit their view of what they accomplish (62%)
- Owning their success (61%)
- Knowing they are meant to have a seat at the table / taking risks (49%)

Where do you stand? Not only are we as women confident, capable, competent, curious, intelligent, beautiful, persuasive, influential, powerful, educated and successful in our own right; we are committed to working extremely hard at the office, in our communities as well as in our homes. While our accolades and accomplishments are infinite, we unfortunately face daily adversaries that hinder us more than we realize: how society views us (what we can't control) and how we view ourselves (what we have 100% control over).

Society says:

- You have to look a certain way
- You have to be a certain size (Please don't get me started on "revenge bodies"; as if women can't lose weight because they love themselves vs proving their attractiveness to external parties)
- Men should earn more than women for equal work
- Your success must equate to some antiquated "one size fits all mentality" that typically forces you to choose unnecessarily between your profession and your family

What we tell ourselves:

- I don't have the education/credentials
- I'm not _____ enough
- I have to be perfect (and so do the conditions) before I make the first step
- I don't have what "it" takes

What society **doesn't** say is:

- You can have a phenomenal career AND a wonderful family
- You should play bigger because you're capable AND because you deserve the best
- You should define professional success on your own terms

- Women are leaders - with or without a "leadership title" (Side Note: always leverage your skills and experiences in a way that benefits your career)
- Perfectionism is the enemy of progress

So, who am I? I'm glad you asked:

- I am incredibly optimistic, full of faith and willing to pursue success alone if need be
- I am building a legacy and making my family proud one day at a time
- I am imperfect yet I'm the best version of me you'll ever meet
- I love Jesus and listen to Jay Z
- I graduated from college at 40 (after 22 years of inconsistent class attendance)
- I transitioned into industries where I lacked formal education and experience because I positioned myself properly on paper (my resume) as well as in person (the interview)
- I am the retired "Queen of Comfort Zone" and planner who had no plan for most of her career
- My titles include: Career Consultant, Adjunct Professor, Professional Development Officer, Career Columnist, Author and Aunt "Chubby"

Last but certainly not least, I am adamant about women communicating their value, earning their worth and believing they are worthy. Know this going forward:

(1) It is possible to succeed at work in a way that best serves you
(2) I'm here to help you ditch imperfection, play bigger and make PowHer Moves in your career

This book serves as the sign, confirmation and encouragement you seek to defy society's definition of who you should be. In the words of Mahatma Gandhi, "I will not let anyone walk through my mind with their dirty feet." These dirty feet in cute stilettos include society's limitations and the negative thoughts that undermine your success. You can expect PowHer Principles and actionable PowHer Moves throughout this book that stretch you beyond your comfort zone ultimately inspiring you to play bigger in your career. Now, without further ado ladies…let's persevere, plan for success, play to win and make PowHer Moves!

Sincerely,

Ericka

Table of Contents

PowHer Principle #1

It Begins With You

"I am fearfully and wonderfully made."

~ PSALM *139:14*

While facilitating a recent workshop, one of the attendees shared "I told the Recruiter, I just want you to know up front, I lack …" and proceeded to fully disclose her weaknesses as well as the requirements she did NOT meet for an available position. When I asked why she felt compelled to share this information with the Recruiter, she stated "I wanted her to know." While, this was a component of her truth- it wasn't the truth in its entirety. Truth is subjective and based on the individual's perspective; fact on the other hand is rooted in results. She was guilty of what I and countless other women have been guilty of: leading from our inadequacies and weaknesses. Unfortunately, she was desperate to land something; anything because she needed a job like yesterday. Her lack of confidence and negative self-perception showed up as "I just wanted her to know". I looked at her, smiled ever so gently and said "Never lead from your weaknesses. You have 15+ years in IT (Information Technology), are considered an expert in your field based on your knowledge as well as your experience, therefore I need you to communicate from that space." I yearned for her to focus on her results in conjunction with the contributions she's made in the industry. I longed for her to stop confirming what society has whispered in the ears of women for decades which is similar to what the financial services industry says to countless accounts on a daily basis: "You are insufficient." Although she is fearfully and wonderfully made, the decision to disregard ownership of this principle produced plenty of interviews but no solid job offers. Whatever you decide to focus on expands (positive or negative) and manifests in your life, so remember:

- Everything you've accomplished professionally and will accomplish begins with the way you see yourself
- Everything you've worked for and everything you haven't worked for is visible in your career results
- Everything you are and everything you're not stems from what you believe about yourself

With this in mind, anything that contradicts the premise you are fearfully and wonderfully made should be disregarded- effective immediately! Being wonderfully made doesn't mean you're perfect nor does it mean you shouldn't improve in certain areas. When you own your strengths, operate in your gifts and understand your individuality, you've actually identified your competitive advantage. It is during those very moments you neglect to magnify your flaws which is EXACTLY where you want to be. In understanding your career begins with you and how your view yourself, every day you must choose to believe in the one person who has the most control over your life: YOU! Instead of fixating on your flaws, talk yourself into success and be accountable for every decision you make that impacts your career.

PowHer *Move*

Communicate your competitive advantage (what you do extremely well and the results) with 3 individuals this week. Then pose a follow up question: "Have I omitted anything that stands out to you?" Make adjustments if you must but own your greatness, one day and one conversation at a time.

PowHer Principle #2

The Dreadful 3 C's

*"Comedians tend to find a comfort zone
and stay there and do lamer versions of
themselves for the rest of their career."*

~ CHRIS ROCK

Although you face external opposition in your career, the 3 C's will leave you stagnant and have you questioning your relevance in the workplace. Even worse, you could remain in your comfort zone like I did for 18 years because you don't recognize the insufficiency of complacent environments. The dreadful 3 C's: conformity, comparisons and comfort are counterproductive thoughts that undermine your ability to achieve greatness in the workplace. Consider the following when addressing the 3 C's in your career:

- Conformity: Transform your role, don't conform i.e. follow the crowd. Consider an issue you can resolve, a process you can improve, a model you can implement that improves the way your organization performs, then position yourself as an expert. Increase your visibility, track your results and get used to being your #1 advocate.

- Comparisons: Clarify your most valued and respected workplace attributes without considering the strengths of others. You can assess the competition while acknowledging your own areas of improvement without negating your own authentic greatness. You have strengths; master a skill if need be and know you are ENOUGH! When you say "_____ is much better at......", it positions you to play from an inferior plane which should never be an option.
- Comfort: Chart a path that details where you see yourself professionally next year, in 3 years, 5 years and 10 years; then see yourself achieving your goals- nothing less and no excuses. Convince yourself failure isn't an option while remaining flexible in your quest to make your career dreams a reality.

PowHer *Move*

Rank comfort, comparisons and conformity with 1 being the least of your worries and 3 being your greatest threat to career success. Implement one action that will change "the dreadful c" you rated a 3 to a 1.

PowHer Principle #3

The Subtle Settle

*"I think happiness is a choice. If you feel yourself
being happy and can settle into the life choices
you make, then it's great. It's really, really great.
I swear to God happiness is the best makeup."*

~ Drew Barrymore

*W*ho doesn't want to be happy in their career? The one
thing that could cause you to be unfulfilled in your profession is your approach to choices. Every day you're bombarded
with this one task that takes on many forms: making a decision. I
read on the internet (and you know it's true if it's on the internet)
that on average, adults make 35,000 decisions per day having
to select this or that. Here's a minute snapshot of what captures
space in our heads from time to time:

- What should I wear?
- What should I eat?
- What do I want?
- Should I apply for the job?

- Should I ask for the raise?
- Should I tell my boss I'm overwhelmed?
- Should I risk it all to pursue what I love?

Here's how you fall for the "subtle settle": as you continue to make decisions throughout your day, you drain your willpower. The risk associated with this is called decision fatigue and it's costing you more than you realize. Effects of decision fatigue include: impulsive decisions, ineffective results or sometimes you simply do nothing courtesy of depleted energy. At what point do you channel your mental energy into making the most productive decisions that aid in goal achievement? When do you stop settling for responding to every thought that invades your mental space?

I suggest leveraging these strategies:

- Delegation: Who is capable of handling this task? Give it to them...fully give it to them and remove yourself as much as possible
- Impulsiveness: weigh the first option you're given and decide. Don't spend the majority of the day toiling with 3 options. Use your lifeline, solicit advice or just do it and learn along the way
- Prioritization: place the most energy and thought into decisions that have the greatest impact
- Reflection: What did you do well? What didn't go well? Where can you improve?

PowHer *Move*

On your busiest day of the work week, assess your choices and analyze your results at the end of your day. What should you say no to? Make the necessary adjustments in your decision-making process so you will have the energy necessary to consistently lead with your best self. Less is more when you consider making the best decisions that yield greater impact.

PowHer Principle #4

Kiss My "But" Goodbye

"He who controls others may be powerful but he who has mastered himself is mightier still."

~ LAO TZU

Did the latter part of Lao Tzu's quote resonate with you? If so, is it because you're a fan of self-mastery or because you naturally focus on what's communicated after "but"? But has been referred to as a verbal landmine that demolishes the effect you are attempting to create. I've certainly found this to be true from personal experience. Women engage in and initiate conversations that reduce their credibility as well as their contribution on a daily basis thanks to their "but". Unfortunately, your "but" could be the reason you're not playing bigger or are perceived as someone who isn't prepared for upward mobility within the organization.

Below you'll find subtle examples that downplay, undervalue and lessen your true workplace worth:

- *I'm qualified for the Strategy Manager role but my resume isn't indicative of that.*
- *Overall my performance was good, but clearly not good enough since my rating was average.*
- *I want to study Information Systems but I'm not as young as I used to be.*

Let's rethink and restate shall we:

- *I'm qualified for the Strategy Manager role so I'm updating my resume and applying for the job this evening.*
- *My performance rating was average.*
- *I want to study Information Systems which requires an adjustment on my part.*

I replaced but with and, removed but altogether and found yet another replacement for but (which).

PowHer *Move*

Your listener could potentially focus on everything you've communicated after "but". Consider eliminating "but" or replacing it with the sole objective of conveying confidence and competence.

PowHer Principle #5

It's An Inside Job

"Self-esteem is what we think, feel and believe about ourselves. Self-worth is recognizing I am greater than all those things."

~ DR. CHRISTINA HIBBERT

*Y*ou've been evaluating yourself since you were in elementary school and will more than likely continue to do so. The way you see yourself is an influential predictor of the results you are currently experiencing in your career- whether positive or negative. I had no idea perfectionism was considered a characteristic of low self-esteem until I conducted research for this book. In Deb Muoio's study "Dangerous Dualities: Perfectionism and Low Self-Esteem", she concludes people with poor self-image have a greater tendency of setting unreasonably high expectations of themselves and for others.

Although low self-esteem can result from socioeconomic status, self-criticism, external opinions, internal perceptions, physical appearance and weight, I've yet to meet a woman who hasn't asked herself, "Am I _____ enough?" If you've ever felt over-worked, experienced perfectionism, discounted accolades or un-dermined your achievements, subconsciously you could be a high achiever who struggles with Imposter Syndrome- a woman who doesn't believe she deserves her success. With approximately 70% of the population being affected with Imposter Syndrome, I felt it was worthy of mentioning- especially when I understand women who are impacted by it could be plagued with low self-confidence, anxiety, stress and depression. You can no longer af-ford to allow thoughts of inferiority to stunt your career growth; you must manage what's happening on the inside.

This principle serves as a reminder that a healthy self-esteem is available and sustainable for every woman who acknowledges she's worthy of experiencing abundance. The principle serves as encouragement to understand you are the sole controller of your thoughts; that every day you have an opportunity to improve and play bigger, therefore you should- unapologetically!

PowHer *Move*

Choose one the following to elevate or sustain your self-esteem, then incorporate a specific action to implement for 30 consecutive days.

- Firmly believe in your values, vision and mission for your career (Today is a great day to identify your values, vision and mission if you haven't)
- Celebrate yourself by way of affirmations, reviewing accomplishments, etc.
- Avoid comparisons
- Unlearn negative thoughts you've learned that you currently hold as truth; replace them with positive thoughts
- Compliment yourself
- Believe you are worthy of success

PowHer Principle #6

Clarity

"The best way to succeed is to have a specific Intent, a clear Vision, a plan of Action, and the ability to maintain Clarity. Those are the Four Pillars of Success. It never fails!"

~ STEVE MARABOLI

Over the years as I've coached clients to career success, the one thing that impedes their progress more than a lack of confidence is the lack of clarity. The candidates who state "I'm desperate. I'll take anything at this point" are typically greeted with my infamous follow-up question, "What specific role would you like to secure?" The reason for this is simple:

- No specific role identified means no targeted resume for the role you're interested in
- No targeted resume for the role you're interested in will drastically decrease opportunities for interviews
- Decreased opportunities for interviews equate to limited opportunities for job offers

By simply knowing what you want, you can begin to make progress in your career. I say you can begin to make progress because that's only a portion of the clarity puzzle. While you must get clear on what you want, you should also know what's holding you back, who is holding you back and who has your back.

When I surveyed clients who schedule complimentary Career Chats with me, I was appalled while analyzing the results. The data provided me with clarity and I now understand why my work pertaining to career strategy, career support and interview mastery is critical to the professional success of women:

- 50% indicate their interviewing skills are average (keep in mind no one hires average talent so you can't afford to have average interviewing skills. Feel free to enroll in my complimentary training EPIC Interviews; the link can be accessed via a pinned post on my Facebook Page @ConfidentCareerWoman)
- 60% lack confidence
- 70% need ongoing career support and advice
- 80% need to identify their next career move
- 80% neglect to update their resume monthly

Billy Cox said it best: "Clarity is power. The more clear you are about what you want, the more likely you are to achieve it."

PowHer *Move*

Make a list of external factors standing in your way of career progression such as unequal pay, sexism, racism and the economy, then throw the list away! As long as you focus on what you can't control, you don't challenge yourself to change, grow and think innovatively.

Make 3 columns with the following headings: what's holding me back, who's holding me back and who has my back. Evaluate what you've captured in each column, then decide how you should proceed, with whom and take action.

PowHer Principle #7

Ditch The Downplay

"Our deepest fear is not that we are inadequate. Our deepest fear is that we are powerful beyond measure. It is our light, not our darkness that most frightens us. We ask ourselves, Who am I to be brilliant, gorgeous, talented and fabulous? Actually, who are you not to be? You are a child of God. Your playing small does not serve the world. There is nothing enlightened about shrinking so that other people will not feel insecure around you."

~ MARIANNE WILLIAMSON

*A*s of 2016, women earned more PhD's than men- and that's for 8 consecutive years in a row; 57.4 % have graduate degrees vs 42.6 % of men and 30% of women have bachelor's degrees (one percentage point greater than men). Women contribute massive value to the workplace (with or without a degree) and we can no longer be shy when it comes to communicating the facts to support this notion. This principle simply acknowledges that although women are more educated than men in certain instances, poorly represented talent challenges within organizations hold women back. Therefore, we shouldn't downplay our contribution and commit to holding ourselves back as well. I understand there are instances when we as women feel inadequate even though we're qualified. Been there; done that. Because I didn't obtain my bachelor's degree until I was 40, I had to draw a line in the sand early in my career and ask myself: "Although I'm smart and capable, will I play to win or shall I remove myself from the game because everyone appears to be more educated than I?"

Turn to your neighbor and say "She opted to play and win." No two women have the same skill set, education and experience but every woman can make the conscious choice to stop downplaying their credibility and/or their credentials. Every woman has the option to say "You hired me for my valuable contribution and I'm determined to produce nothing less than what you've selected me to do." With this in mind, dare to excel without showcasing your (perceived) shortcomings.

PowHer *Move*

Women aren't socialized to own their strengths. In some instances, women play small as it relates to their expertise and it's to our detriment in the workplace. This week, schedule a meeting with your leader and prepare to discuss 3 of your greatest accomplishments over the past 6 months, including the quantitative results (value to the organization). During the session, discuss who you can collaborate with on an upcoming short-term project that leverages your expertise and increases your visibility.

PowHer Principle #8

Mask On, Mask Off

*"Even though I had sold 70 million albums,
there I was feeling like "I'm no good at this."*

~ JENNIFER LOPEZ

In 2011, Jennifer Lopez was named the World's Most Beautiful Woman by People Magazine, which was her mask on moment. On the contrary, behind closed doors she questioned her capabilities in her career – after selling 70 million albums! This was her reality; the moment when her mask was authentically off. Women face similar struggles on a daily basis and can relate to J-Lo's sentiment I'm sure. Although we may not have the star status of J-Lo, we sometimes select a mask for work and for social media that isn't consistent with what our true reality is.

On 8/25/17, my father was in a car accident. Shortly thereafter, he was diagnosed with brain damage. When his life changed, mine did as well. Instantaneously I became his medical power of attorney from another state. As a result, I made frequent trips to VA to support him during this critical time. Between 8/26 - 10/1,

I'd spent 22 days in VA while juggling the demands of maintaining my business, balancing full-time employment in addition to my then Adjunct Professor role in a different state. I was starting to fall apart, one fragile thread at a time (mask off). If you were following me on social media during that time, you had no idea (mask on). What you saw was the new book cover, updated images for my new website launch, articles I'd written, posts relevant to workshops I was facilitating, career advice and pictures from my mini vacation in the Bahamas. The cost of the mask and the demands of my father's health showed up as a nervous reaction in my lower lip, watery eyes, headaches, reduced sleep and irregular menstrual cycles. I eventually told myself "You need to make different choices and one of those choices is acknowledging you don't have everything together. Everything isn't a priority nor should it be."

While vacationing in the Bahamas, I had lunch with my Coach (Doreen Rainey). She shared wisdom, advice and guidance that allowed me to slowly remove the mask relating to my business. I then took subsequent steps to minimize the stress in my life and remove the mask in my personal life. Please understand progress doesn't require perfection but it does require prioritization. You can't do it all nor should you decide to – especially all at once.

PowHer *Move*

If there's a discrepancy between your happiness as a professional and your personal happiness (when you're away from work), this is a clear indicator you may need to shift or consult a trusted advisor.

Ideally, you should always place your oxygen mask on before helping others but understand the burden of an oxygen mask, a work mask and a personal mask just isn't worth bearing.

PowHer Principle #9

IT'S ALL YOU!!

"Competence brings confidence."

~ ANONYMOUS

Abraham Maslow, the Father of Psychology penned "A Theory of Human Motivation". He discussed self-actualization which occurs when you maximize your potential; when you're doing the absolute best you're capable of doing. Ladies, may I have your attention please? The virtual playing field has officially been leveled! Each of us on any given day can do our best as we are all on the road to "becoming" in our careers. We are competent and can choose to be confident. Even when we experience moments of uncertainty, Maslow anticipated our needs by understanding limits are self-imposed. He offers clarity as he described self-actualized individuals below:

- They accept themselves, together with all their flaws
- They are not troubled by the small things (they focus on the big picture)
- Self-actualized people are not perfect

- They share deep relationships with a few, but also feel identification and affection towards the entire human race
- Self-actualized people are grateful

I dare not question your competence. However, I must pose the real question which is: "Are you self-actualized or have you allowed perfectionism to hinder you professionally?"

PowHer *Move*

Love and accept yourself, flaws and all! If there are aspects of your life that require change to make you happier, healthier, wiser and smarter, by all means set realistic goals to incorporate the necessary adjustments. Don't stop progressing professionally because you think you're not _____ enough.

PowHer Principle #10

Continuous Learning And Unlearning

"For me, education was power."

~ MICHELLE OBAMA

I've read "to earn more you must learn more" but no one ever told me I needed continuous learning in conjunction with unlearning. To unlearn means "to discard something learned, especially a bad habit or false, outdated information from one's memory." The best example I can think of is how the internet changed the hiring process, injecting global competition amongst candidates and how branding is now an essential part of your career toolkit.

Early in my career, I would visit employers before noon in a dark navy or black suit when seeking employment opportunities. I'd complete my paper application, sometimes interview on the spot and receive a job offer in less than 3 business days on average. Needless to say, I've had to unlearn certain aspects of the process because I can now apply for openings online. I've had to learn how to manage social media profiles while staying abreast of resume and interviewing trends. I've had to build relationships, expand my network, conduct employer-related research and discover my competitive advantage. What will you need to unlearn to take your career to the next level? Perhaps there's something you need to unlearn personally that's hindering your professional growth or your ability to earn more.

Or at least that's been my experience…..Because I've set a personal goal of becoming the first millionaire in my family, I needed to challenge my thoughts and perspectives regarding money. Trust me, my financial blueprint was a factor that resulted in how much money I accepted (and left on the table) annually in my career. I didn't grow up wealthy so I wasn't exposed to passive income, multiple revenue streams, the financial rewards of entrepreneurship nor investments. My grandparents experienced segregation, they have a middle school education, my mother was born in 1950 and one of my great aunts is still "The Help" in 2017. Simply securing employment as well as an education was a tremendous blessing during those times so needless to say my family wasn't exposed to financial wealth. I had to make a conscious decision to learn more and to change my mindset beyond my environment which influenced my reality. Your commitment to continuous learning will be the game changer in your career, just as challenging my money mind map was for me. With this in mind make time to read, listen to a podcast or audiobook, complete coursework or watch a video series so you can utilize the applied knowledge to accelerate and sustain your career success.

PowHer *Move*

Your success is defined by you, not what others would have you believe. Define your career success without limitations; your ideal salary, position, employer as well as your geographic location. Now what will you need to learn and unlearn to achieve your goal?

PowHer Principle #11

No Goals, No Greatness

"Write the vision and make it plain; though it tarry, wait for it because it will surely come."

~ HABAKKUK 2: 2-3

Harvard Business Study says 14% of those with goals are 10 times more successful than those without them.

The 3% with written goals were 3 times more successful than the 14% with unwritten goals. If there's one mistake I've made in my career, it was spending most of it without a plan. I experienced a degree of growth because I was often recruited by competitors which is a blessing in and of itself. Without a plan, I have to admit my growth was also significantly stunted. The results from my surveyed clients who schedule complimentary Career Chats confirm that professional women feel stuck yet they are still neglecting to plan for career success:

- 40% feel stuck in their career
- 70% have no development plan in place

- 80% don't have a career strategy
- 100% are in need of a social capital strategy (networking)

Now is the time to unleash the power of planning, especially when you consider the benefits: focus, motivation, measurability and increased employee worth. To assist women with planning their career success, I've designed a PowHer Career Journal which allows you to create career targets, identify perceived obstacles, pinpoint necessary partners and track accomplishments. Not only can you leverage the journal for performance reviews and appraisals, you can refer to it when updating your resume or preparing for interviews. To order your journal, visit ErickaSpradley.com or contact us: info@erickaspradley.com

PowHer *Move*

Write down your top 3 work priorities for the next 12 months. These priorities should align with your definition of career success from PowHer Principle #10; next specify one action for each priority then add your completion date for each action.

Smart women such as yourself leverage the power of SMART Goals: specific, measurable, attainable, relative and time-bound.

PowHer Principle #12

Amplify!

"I'm here for purpose, precision and peak performance not a popularity contest."

~ ERICKA SPRADLEY

When you amplify, you automatically turn up, magnify, intensify, increase, boost and step up. This should consistently be the standard for your performance. I love Jay Z's thoughts regarding performance: "Excellence is being able to perform at a high level for a long period of time. You can hit a half-court shot once, that's just luck of the draw. If you can do it consistently, that's excellence." Are you a luck of the draw performer at work or do you exemplify amplified excellence?

Throughout my career, any leader I had the pleasure of working for will tell you:

I'm reliable, proactive, hard-working, trustworthy, I perform well (exceed expectations), am positive, that I have a stellar reputation and that I resolve problems. I've consistently demonstrated these favorable workplace traits for 20+ years. I amplified my strengths and will continue to do so. Amplification for me isn't an option but is the standard that has allowed me to make one PowHer Move after another in my career. Whether I was transitioning upward, navigating horizontally, changing industries or making lateral strides, I was concerned with performance (mine as well as those who reported to me) because ultimately, that's what I was hired to do.

Aside from my performance in conjunction with amplification, another ingredient of my career success is my obsession with preparation.

It doesn't matter if I'm facilitating material or content I've taught many times over, I practice – then I practice again, then I practice some more. There's a correlation between preparedness, confidence and performance. If your intent is to amplify; to play bigger in your career, consider increasing your level of preparedness which is so much more than simply updating your resume and anticipating an interview. Preparation is what you do before a meeting, at the end of your workday or in those moments during your commute. It's essentially a lifestyle. Career success doesn't just happen- you prepare by being ready and when you stay ready, you don't have to get ready.

PowHer *Move*

Proactively analyze your department for signs of impending change with the intent to amplify your performance. Be aware of organizational priorities one level above your title and one level below. How can you amplify your performance (more effectively and more efficiently) in a way that multiples your results?

PowHer Principle #13

Drop F-Bombs

There are 3 F-Bombs you should consistently assess in your career: follow-up, feedback and fear.

"I always like to plan ahead and follow-up."

~ MICHAEL JACKSON

The King of Pop (my first boyfriend) Michael Jackson was a planner who followed up and was known around the world for his performance. If planning and follow up were present behind the scenes in conjunction with his work ethic, here's what the results yielded:

- 750M albums sold world-wide
- 48 Albums charted on Billboard (he was 51 only years old when he died)
- For 5 consecutive years in a row, he's the top earning deceased celebrity with $75M annually

F-Bomb # 1: Follow-up: When you follow up, it shows you're reliable, interested, caring, serious, it sets you apart and makes the recipient feel valued. There's no downside to following up (unless you follow up too much and annoy the recipient). Why not reap the benefits of counteracting those who "drop the ball" by choosing to follow up during the course of your work week? Follow-up isn't a mere to do item on your checklist, it's a key ingredient of memorable impressions and tremendous impact (performance/reputation) as we can clearly see in the legendary legacy of Michael Jackson.

> *"It's a challenge to grow professionally and move up the corporate ladder when you're not receiving feedback on your performance."*

> ~ JOHN RAMPTON

F-Bomb # 2: Feedback (aka the breakfast of champions): Seek it, ask for it and apply when needed. As you are probably aware, all feedback isn't valuable nor comfortable -especially when you were giving your best or thought you were meeting performance expectations. However, feedback is one of the greatest gifts you can receive in your career. How will you know what behaviors to adjust without it? How will you know how to decrease efforts that undermine efficiency? How will you know when you're doing extraordinarily well in the office? When properly administered, feedback is a tool for continued learning; it can be motivating and can certainly enhance your performance.

Bill Gates said it best, "We all need people who will give us feedback. That's how we improve."

*"I've learned that fear limits you and your vision.
It serves as blinders to what may be just a few
steps down the road for you. The journey is
valuable, but believing in your talents, your
abilities, and your self-worth can empower you to
walk down an even brighter path. Transforming
fear into freedom - how great is that?"*

~ SOLEDAD O'BRIEN

F-Bomb #3: Fear: Whether it's fear of failure or fear of change, you can expect both of them to undermine your career success EVERY time. Jack Canfield says "confronting your fears is a very necessary step in achieving success, there's simply no other way." I couldn't agree more. I like most people was terrified of public speaking for most of my life. I can remember a few short years ago while on a conference call, I experienced butterflies in my stomach. I wasn't on stage, speaking to an audience – I WAS ON THE PHONE!

The turning point for me was actually more like a cross country journey, nevertheless I was determined to overcome my phobia. I read "God hasn't given you a spirit of fear" followed by "fear is made up." Then I joined Toastmasters. However, it wasn't until my purpose revealed I am obligated to share my expertise and experiences with others so they can experience career success that I became even more desperate to confront my fear. The final destination on my fearful public speaking journey was a mentoring session with Maggie Mistal. She said "When did you first realize you were afraid to speak in public?" I traveled back in time to the kid in elementary school who was afraid to stand on stage and speak to the audience of adults attending a PTA Meeting in Newport

News, VA. Unbeknownst to me, I'd carried that fearful little girl with me throughout my career. Maggie served as my Soledad; the one who helped me transform fear into freedom and I can say with a 100% certainty that freedom is much better than fear- hands down.

PowHer *Move*

Which F-Bomb will you drop this week so you can play bigger: follow up, feedback or fear?

PowHer Principle #14

Discipline

"Effective leadership is putting first things first. Effective management is discipline, carrying it out."

~ Stephen Covey

There was a study conducted several years ago titled "The Underrepresentation of African-American Women In Executive Leadership: What's Getting In The Way?". It states:

- Women must know what they want (develop a career plan)
- Women must be willing to accept leadership positions in order to demonstrate their competencies and skill sets to senior leaders (By the way, if you haven't been tapped for a project, ask for the assignment leveraging PowHer Principle #19)
- Women must take responsibility for their careers

Not only do you have to manage your career, you have to take total responsibility for it – even in the absence of those who should support you. One of the ways you take responsibility for your career is by incorporating discipline and habits that take your career to the next level.

Daily:

- Produce quality work, go the extra mile and strive to exceed expectations. Nowadays average is extremely common so in the eyes of many, it's acceptable. What matters is your leader's performance expectation so be clear on what that is vs what you perceive. You want to give your best effort consistently, learn from your mistakes and seek feedback for continued growth.
- Take 5 min to track your success, then create a Success Document. You can reference your document for performance evaluation conversations as well as interview preparation.

Weekly:

- Capture 3 specific examples of your results that demonstrate skill proficiency and add them to your Success Document including who, what, when, why and which skills were leveraged. Whether it's taking the lead on a project or participating in one, you should have documentation detailing the situation, your actions and the result. Affirming your result-driven accomplishments serves as encouragement and also confirms your value to the organization. This document should be referenced for interview preparation, monthly meetings with your leader and performance conversations.

- Absorb new information. Knowledge is the new currency and continuous learning aids in your professional growth. Keep in mind you should also self- assess as well. Ask yourself "What will I need to start doing, what should I stop doing and what should I continue doing?"; then implement a plan of action.

Monthly:

- Meet with your mentor and/or your leader. Arrive prepared to discuss performance, ideas, business trends and ask questions. Allow these meetings to not only serve as accountability but to also help you course correct when needed.
- Express gratitude. Whether it's a thank you or agreeing to mentor someone, express appreciation and be willing to serve as you climb the ladder of career success.

PowHer *Move*

Because you are the product of your habits, I recommend eliminating one habit that's hindering your performance or professional progress. It's easy to implement another (new) habit but sometimes our ineffectiveness has little to do with ability and more to do with being overextended. Subtract before you add.

PowHer Principle #15

Track What You Treasure

*"Monitor your progress and your
calendar as if your career life depends
on it because in actuality, it does! "*

~ ERICKA SPRADLEY

My former leader used to say "Spradley, if it isn't in black and white, it doesn't exist." I dreaded having conversations about "the business" and our numbers because I couldn't seem to get my point across. If I can be totally transparent, there was a deficit in my ability to lead. Those conversations exposed my weakness as a leader which led to feelings of inadequacy. Instead of wallowing in my weakness, I approached it as a challenge. In order to play bigger, I had to elevate my preparation strategy as it pertained to our meetings in conjunction with my approach for analyzing the numbers. Eventually, I came to appreciate those meetings because I became a savvy leader in the process. Once I unleashed the power of tracking, my relationship with my performance improved. I tracked sales, questioned past trends, predicted future revenues, leveraged talent during peak times and adjusted inventory levels. By doing so, my store not only received recognition, it also experienced record sales growth! One of my greatest career lessons is simple: monitor and track your progress. Never should you ever show up to a meeting with anyone without knowing your metrics and how your performance impacts the departmental/organizational goals. My rationale behind this is you can't communicate your value when you haven't identified your impact.

When understanding your impact, ask yourself the following:

- What are your key activities?
- How do you help (your value, contribution, etc.)?
- What skills do you possess that drive results?

When monitoring and tracking your performance, know that it helps you:

- Focus so you can move toward the direction of your goals
- Identify which activities produce the best results
- Eliminate what isn't working
- Think innovatively to achieve greater results

Not only do you have to manage your time as well as your career, you have to take total responsibility for it meaning what does and does not transpire. Your chances of success increase dramatically when you evaluate the business, self-assess, eliminate obstacles, resolve problems, document/ track your progress and manage your time.

Here are my top 3 calendar hacks to give you more time in your day to monitor and track your performance:

- Respond to email less frequently: Just because a message arrives in your inbox doesn't mean it's a priority. Trust me, you can respond to some of your emails at the end of the day or within 24 hours unless there's an urgent matter requiring your attention
- Identify time wasters: Does this take more time initially? Yes. Will it save you time in the long-run? YES! This could be a task that someone else should focus on or procrastination on your part. Either way, the goal is to maximize efficiency and productivity without consistently wasting time
- Do not disturb: If your phone has push notifications or your computer has instant messaging capability, you may need to manage your distractions to find more time in your day. It may not be necessary to silence your phone completely, but once you consider sidebar conversations, social media breaks, text messages and the like, you can lose 30 min/day easily. By the end of any given work week, you've lost 2.5 hours of productivity

PowHer *Move*

Identify one goal, track your results for 14 days and rate your progress over the 2-week period. Give yourself the grace to adjust along the way. The idea is accelerated goal achievement, to course correct and celebrate your small wins so you can leverage them as motivation to go further faster.

PowHer Principle #16

Emotional Intelligence

"Your intellect may be confused but your emotions will never lie to you."

~ ROGER EBERT

 motional intelligence is your ability to recognize your emotions and the emotions of others; it is your ability to discern between different feelings while labeling them appropriately. There's actually a Harvard Business Review article from 2015 titled "How Emotional Intelligence Became A Key Leadership Skill" that states without emotional intelligence, a person can have the best training in the world, an incisive, analytical mind and an endless supply of smart ideas but (s)he won't make a great leader. I'm willing to go out on a limb and say that if you're not emotionally smart, your PowHer Moves will be limited. Women who possess emotional intelligence play the career game on a different level.

- They understand themselves; they know what their triggers are and why
- They control outbursts, impulses and manage their emotions
- They understand others
- They manage their relationships (how they interact with others)
- They observe non-verbal communication
- They are open-minded, meaning they don't creatively assume and then honor it as truth
- They empathize

Although the KMPG Women's Leadership Study lists confidence, critical thinking, decision making, interviewing and negotiation as some of the skills needed to move women into leadership, I can assure you you'll need emotional intelligence as well.

PowHer *Move*

Commit to abandoning the following traits that inhibit your ability to develop the key leadership skill of emotional intelligence: complaining, negativity, dwelling on past events and criticism. In addition, you also want to monitor your interactions with others who possess these traits lest you are convicted and labeled guilty by association.

PowHer Principle #17

I Run This

"Once you get a bad reputation, there's nothing you can do about it."

~ My Momma

*F*or context purposes, my sweet Mother was referring to the "fast girl at summer camp" but nevertheless, this one success principle helped me create advocates, sponsors and mentors who have supported me throughout my career.

If there's one thing that accelerated my professional progress aside from my performance and commitment to preparation, it would have to be my reputation aka "my brand".

Because you are the only person responsible for your career, that makes you the boss; the one who manages "the enterprise" meaning you are the woman who is running things. This responsibility of running things includes the task of managing your reputation. The invisible interview is REAL; it is causing people to lose their jobs, it is ongoing and not merely reserved for your scheduled appointment to discuss your next career move. Everything from what you say to your social media presence is being observed. Career progression nowadays is so much more than performance; it not only includes your image and reputation, you must also remain relevant, take risks and by all means learn to relax.

Relevance: Leadership has unfortunately been reduced to a title in the minds of some. The danger in doing so means we disregard some of our most valuable employees – especially individual contributors who at some point will start to question their value as well as their relevance. If you're questioning your relevance or struggling to stay relevant, know that you should consistently:

- Raise your hand to take the lead on projects to increase your visibility and broaden your skill set
- Make yourself a resource for others
- Adapt
- Innovate
- Peruse the intranet to keep your finger on the pulse of what's happening in the organization
- Read the annual report
- Expand and sustain your network
- Understand future trends
- Research the industry and your employer's competitors

Risk: At some point in your career, you're faced with the inevitable "Should I go for it?" with the full understanding that charging ahead forces you into the unknown and sometimes a world of discomfort. On the other hand, not taking a risk is considered a risk! If you want to increase your visibility or advance your career, be the catalyst for helping your department accelerate change with the understanding calculated risks can serve you well. Consider the following when you assess risk:

- How will you frame the risk (project)?
- How will you minimize risk?
- Who can you tap for support?
- What incremental steps can you take to develop momentum?

Relax: Career management or lack thereof can be exhausting. Because you run this, you're no stranger to running errands, running from meeting to meeting or feeling as though things are running awry. When demands experience competition, it's easy to find yourself stretched thin and agitated. Who you don't want to become is the attitudinal, impulsive, angry, inconsistent, stressed woman in the office, so do yourself a favor and relax on a regular basis. This could mean opting out of meetings, choosing 3 essential priorities and eliminating the rest, mini-meditations, taking breaks (especially lunch away from your desk), resisting the urge to multi-task, finding your flow or taking time off to recharge.

PowHer *Move*

What 3 actions will you take to incorporate self-care? Taking care of yourself and making yourself a priority isn't selfish contrary to what we tell ourselves. When you prioritize self-care, you have the headspace to relax, take risks and remain relevant while running things in your career.

PowHer Principle #18

The I's Have It

"I don't care what everyone else is doing, you do what's right."

~ BERTHA DAVIS (MY GRANDMOTHER)

Navigating your career is more than showing up and doing the work. Experiencing professional success encompasses who you are personally at your core meaning your influence, integrity, ideas and intent will determine how others perceive you in the workplace. The I's are a determining factor of how quickly doors will open (and close) when you're attempting to play bigger and make PowHer Moves. How many times have you scrolled online and read about a fallen exec who made one unethical decision too many? How many times have you watched the news only to hear about someone who compromised their integrity to increase revenue?

While I highly recommend keeping your eyes on the prize, I also suggest incorporating these I's to catapult your career to the next level:

- Influence: It comes in multiple forms and can extend vertically or horizontally. It is also your presence and actions that change the attitudes or behaviors among colleagues and direct reports. You have influence but the question is how are you using it to positively impact the trajectory of your career?
- Integrity is your truth. It is also your moral and ethical compass that can only be abandoned by the choices you make. When you walk in integrity, not only do you have the opportunity to extend your influence, you also create trust with colleagues.
- Intellectual capital is an asset. It is the value of your knowledge and training that provides the company with a competitive advantage. It is your ideas, expertise and skills. It is a combination of your education as well as your experience that must be tapped as you contemplate next steps in your career. When you can articulate the correlation between the contribution of your intellectual capital and the impact to the company's bottom line, you will then position yourself to experience a shift in your career.
- Intentionality means to mentally determine some action or result. Simply put, it is knowing what you want and knowing what you don't want. If the goal is to experience career success, you must be intentional. You must make a decision, define your career goals, remain focused and execute - period.

PowHer *Move*

The one I that didn't make the list is inconsistency. Of the 4 I's listed above, which one are you leveraging the least? Note your "Inconsistent I" then commit to consistency in one area that's negatively impacting your career.

PowHer Principle #19

Stop Sitting On Your Ask

*"If you want something said, ask a man; if
you want something done, ask a woman."*

~ MARGARET THATCHER

As soon as you accept a job offer with an organization, you've signed up to play "the game". With this in mind, you should always play to win. The goal is to stay winning which means you must possess the courage to ask for what you want. We can no longer afford to talk ourselves out of our professional desires by assuming the response will be "no." As women, we don't ask for:

- Additional training/professional development
- A flexible schedule
- Special projects that stretch beyond our expertise
- Additional resources
- More money
- Promotions

- Mentors and Sponsors
- Access to Senior Leadership

One tactic you can use when considering your ask is to create mutual wins. Think options and strategy when preparing as well as how both parties will benefit from "the ask". Consider these key questions while paying close attention to the details when positioning your ask:

1. When are you willing to walk away?
2. What is a win in the mind of the person you're asking?
3. How will you close your ask on a high note?

Once you've done your homework, present your win-win ask with the understanding there's a 50/50 chance you'll receive your yes.

Another tactic that I use daily is belief because it builds confidence in your ask. Belief in yourself and believing you will achieve success will shift your career in ways you can't even imagine. Simply put, have faith. My career path nor my journey has worked out the way I thought it would and definitely not on my timetable. However, I wouldn't be who I am nor would I have what I have in the absence of my faith. I've said for years that my business will never fail which stems from my belief that God can (and will) do the impossible; He merely needs me to do my part. My mindset is that should a door close, I'll climb through a window because I refuse to be stopped. When you become a resilient, relentless problem solver with unlimited faith, you identify alternative solutions and continue to make PowHer Moves not because the conditions are right but because you're the right woman for the job.

PowHer *Move*

Asking builds stamina. Within the next 30 days, ask for what you REALLY want, not what you think someone will automatically say yes to. Is it a new assignment, more money, telecommuting options? Build your case in preparation for the conversation and build your stamina as well as your confidence by asking for what you want.

PowHer Principle #20

Complacency

"Comfort is the devil's first cousin."

~ MARC FULLER

I consider comfort an unnecessary evil that I am exceptionally familiar with unfortunately. Today my bio reads well, but that was after 18 years of career complacency and very little planning. I spent 22 years completing a 4-year degree; 18 years in retail and experienced insignificant results with very few career strides.

In less than 10 years, I launched a business, authored 3 books, became an Adjunct Professor, created online courses as well as content for organizations and so on. My career progression in 10 years or less supersedes what I didn't accomplish within the first 18 years of my work experience.

If you're at a place in your career that's seems easy and feels safe, you're in your comfort zone. Therefore, I'm evicting you effective immediately and handing you a relocation package. PowHer

Moves and comfort zones are opposing forces that remind me of Newton's Third Law of Motion: "To every action there exists an equal and opposite reaction." In other words, you're not accelerating if you're comfortable, you're not growing if you're complacent and you definitely can't play bigger when you're stuck.

- Do board rooms make you uncomfortable? Submit an application to serve on a board
- Does speaking in public make you nervous? Ask to present at the next meeting
- Would you like a seat at the table? Don't wait for an invitation; ask the right person the right questions, state your case and request your seat

Here's the recipe for complacency:

- Agility
- Volunteer for stretch projects (and take the lead)
- Create a paradigm shift in your thoughts and desires
- Dare to dream authentically (abandon everyone else's idea of what career success looks like for you)

PowHer *Move*

Schedule an informational interview (15-20 minutes) with your leader's boss or their peer. Conduct your research, have 3-5 questions prepared in advance and be prepared to communicate your value, strengths, impact to the organization and bottom line (your quantitative results)

PowHer Principle #21

Expand

"Playing big doesn't come from working more, pushing harder or finding confidence. It comes from listening to the most powerful and secure part of you, not the voice of self- doubt."

~ TARA MOHR

Did you know your brain tends to focus on one thought at a time? Once it accepts a thought (positive or negative), it works to achieve the outcome of the thought. My challenge to you is to defy your current capacity and stretch beyond the possible (what you see). One of my favorite verses in the Bible is "I walk by faith and not by sight" – 2 Corinthians 5:7. When I hear "that's impossible" I sometimes ask myself "what if it were possible?" I defy capacity. I reject thoughts that are counterproductive to my goals or that contradict where I see myself in the future. I consider solutions and creativity when faced with obstacles. While these things have helped me expand professionally, it would be misleading to paint the picture that I've succeeded on my own.

Because expansion to the next level requires assistance and I can only go so far independently, I hired a Coach.

During a recent session, I communicated my sales results to my coach, she said "What will you need to do to add a zero to that number?" She defied my capacity. When I communicated my 6 month goal to a friend on a Monday, he said "What will you need to do to achieve the goal by Friday?" He defied my capacity.

If you're unsure of how you can expand independently, have people in your life who will help you expand or hire a Coach. Success is never a solo act so you will always need the assistance of others throughout the course of your career to help you reach your next level.

PowHer *Move*

Take 10 minutes of quiet time to determine how you'd like to expand professionally. What changes will you have to make to achieve your expansion goal?

PowHer Principle #22

Competency

*"I have no idols. I admire work,
dedication and competence."*

~ AYRTON SENNA

ompetencies are skills. When you're perceived as competent, there is a belief you can perform efficiently and successfully. However, before you reach peak proficiency or can tout mastery, you must experience the 4 stages of competence:

1. **Unconscious incompetence** is when you don't understand or know how to do something.
2. **Conscious incompetence** occurs when you attempt to learn the skill which of course includes mistakes as an integral part of your learning process.
3. **Conscious competence** is when you understand or know how to do something although demonstrating the skill could require concentration in conjunction with a systematic approach.

4. **Unconscious competence** means the skill has become "second nature" and can be performed easily. During this stage, you can perform the skill while executing another task and even teach others.

Employers understand competencies are needed to create a diverse, talented workforce which of course is key to maintaining the organization's competitive advantage. With this in mind, remember 70-20-10.

- 70% of your competencies should be developed through real-time, on the job experience
- 20% of your competencies should be developed through networking relationships online or in person such as communities of practice
- 10% should be developed through planned training

PowHer *Move*

Pose this question to your leader "What competencies am I lacking that seem to be hindering my career growth?"

PowHer Principle #23

Get Your Money Honey

"Rule #1: Never lose money. Rule #2: Never forget rule #1."

~ WARREN BUFFET

According to a KMPG's Women's Leadership Study, 61% of women don't feel comfortable asking for a raise. As if that number isn't high enough, there's the recent Glassdoor survey indicating women negotiated less than their male counterparts (68% of women didn't negotiate when their salary was offered). I yearn for a day when women not only excel at work but also know their worth and courageously request equal pay for equal contribution. The pay gap will never decrease at the rate we're going if we don't speak up and ask for what we deserve.

When you engage in future salary conversations, know it's totally acceptable to ask what the range is for others in the organization who occupy that role.

Side note: I recommend following the employer's lead meaning give them the professional courtesy to initiate money talk during interviews. Because some employers believe candidates who initiate the salary conversation are focused on "what's in it for them", they don't always "appreciate" qualified candidates who bring up salary first.

The next time an employer extends an offer:

- Do your research which can include what the salary pays in your specific zip code. Data helps you make the best decisions so do your due diligence as you prepare
- Don't be the first to disclose a number. If you must, provide a broad range
- Demonstrate how you add value to the employer's bottom line
- Prepare a counter offer just in case

Lastly, your employer probably has a continuity plan and so should you. I HIGHLY recommend having more than one stream or source of income aside from your employer. I understand not everyone desires entrepreneurship and my desire isn't to persuade you in that direction. My goal is to plant seeds that prepare you to have the income you desire; the balance in your account(s) that meet(s) your needs as well as your wants.

PowHer *Move*

Practice your negotiation skills either with a trusted advisor or when making a purchase. Hone the skill in anticipation of your next salary conversation so you're prepared to confidently discuss dollars. There's no shame in receiving equitable compensation for your expertise that contains multiple zeros and a comma if that's your heart's desire.

PowHer Principle #24

Sleeping Your Way To The Top

*"The advice I would give to my younger self is
very, very simple. Stop burning the candle at both
ends and renew your estranged relationship with
sleep. You'll be more productive, more effective,
more creative and more likely to enjoy your life."*

~ ARIANA HUFFINGTON

Did you know the Center for Disease Control and Prevention said that insufficient sleep is a public health problem? I know social media begs to differ with all of the hustle posts and hastags, people advocating for more work than sleep to achieve your goals and such. However, sleep is vital and a critical component of your success. Ariana is an excellent example of someone who was working extremely hard at one point in her career (18 hour days while building the Huffington Post). Not only was she making PowHer Moves, she also collapsed from exhaustion. In 2007, she was on the phone and checking email when she passed out. As a result, she woke up in a pool of blood with a broken cheekbone and a cut over her eye.

The moral of this principle is if you're going to excel professionally, you need adequate amounts of sleep. I understand you have children, relatives, friends, chores, pets and you even have fun from time to time. You can enjoy yourself personally as well as professionally and STILL sleep well at night. PLEASE remember:

- Sleep can improve productivity and memory
- Sleep can improve your immune function
- Sleep spurs creativity and sharpens attention
- Sleep lowers stress
- Sleep affects emotional and social interactions

PowHer *Move*

Ensure you're sleeping 7-8 hours/night consistently. If a typical night's sleep of 7-8 hours is your exception, more than likely you need new rest rules to enhance your productivity as well as your relationships physically, spiritually, mentally and emotionally.

PowHer Principle #25

It Ends With You

"You alone are enough."

~ Maya Angelou

If you're reading this, believe you're fully capable of playing bigger and making PowHer Moves. I know this with every fiber of my being because you were born with a unique skillset; unmatched talent and unparalleled wisdom. You alone are like no one else on the planet which makes you an asset. Today, I challenge you to manage your career like a business. You are the Chief PowHer Officer who is capable of achieving nothing less than career greatness. Now is the time to use the list below to showcase your "It Factor". That's right; not only will you have your "It" together, from this day forward you will no longer settle for less than you deserve because of self-limiting, defeating thoughts. Nor will you play small, be limited by perfections and imperfections, nor will you hold yourself back.

- Build credibility in the marketplace as well as the workplace
- Create your very own marketing strategy that increases visibility
- Increase revenues for yourself not just your employer
- Plan
- Prepare
- Build and sustain relationships/partnerships
- Collaborate
- Take smarts risks
- Leverage technology
- Examine infrastructure
- Question systems
- Incorporate automation
- Dare to say no thank you
- Excel, be efficient and work with a spirit of excellence

Now is your time to play bigger, make PowHer Moves, walk confidently in the direction of your career dreams and wholeheartedly believe that you are enough. From one Confident Career Woman to another, here's to an elevated mindset, new career goals and major success!!! Cheers!!!

Notes

Statistical Data Resources

1. Intro: KPMG, *"KMPG Women's Leadership Study"*, 2015

2. PowHer Principle #5: Danielle Page, *"How Imposter Syndrome Is Holding You Back"*, Oct. 26, 2017

3. PowHer Principle #6: Ericka Spradley, *"My Next Level Client Study"*, 2016

4. PowHer Principle #7: Mark J. Perry, American Enterprise Institute (AEI) *"Women Earned Majority of Doctoral Degrees in 2016 for 8th Straight Year..."*, Sept. 28, 2017

5. PowHer Principle #11: *"Harvard Written Goals Study 1979"*

6. PowHer Principle #11: Ericka Spradley, *"My Next Level Client Study"*, 2016

7. PowHer Principle # 22: Wendy *"Use the 70-20-10 Model for Your Learning and Development Program*, Sept. 5, 2013

8. PowHer Principle # 23: KPMG, *"KMPG Women's Leadership Study"*, 2015

30223683R00063

Made in the USA
Columbia, SC
03 November 2018